Grumpy Cats
Sweary Color By Numbers Coloring Book
for Adults

ZenMaster Coloring Books

Copyright © 2018 by ZenMaster

All rights reserved. No part of this publication may be reproduced, distributed, or transmitted in any form or by any means, including photocopying, recording, or other electronic or mechanical methods, without the prior written permission of the publisher.

COLOR TEST PAGE

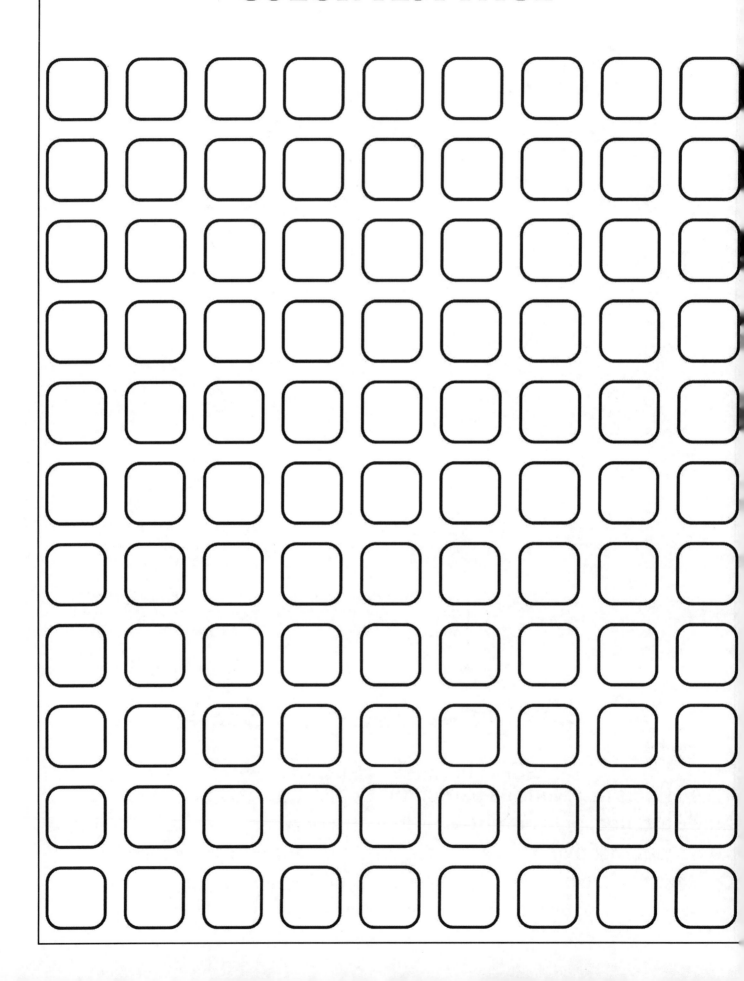

COLOR TEST PAGE

1. Dark Brown
2. Brown
3. Light Brown
4. Tan
5. Khaki
6. Dark Grey
7. Grey
8. Black
9. Light Pink
10. Pink
11. Magenta
12. Purple
13. Yellow
14. Gold
15. Orange
16. Red
17. Lime
18. Palm
19. Green
20. Forest
21. Violet
22. Royal
23. Blue
24. Teal

1. Dark Brown
2. Brown
3. Light Brown
4. Tan
5. Khaki
6. Dark Grey
7. Grey
8. Black
9. Light Pink
10. Pink
11. Magenta
12. Purple
13. Yellow
14. Gold
15. Orange
16. Red
17. Lime
18. Palm
19. Green
20. Forest
21. Violet
22. Royal
23. Blue
24. Teal

1. Dark Brown
2. Brown
3. Light Brown
4. Tan
5. Khaki
6. Dark Grey
7. Grey
8. Black
9. Light Pink
10. Pink
11. Magenta
12. Purple
13. Yellow
14. Gold
15. Orange
16. Red
17. Lime
18. Palm
19. Green
20. Forest
21. Violet
22. Royal
23. Blue
24. Teal

1. Dark Brown
2. Brown
3. Light Brown
4. Tan
5. Khaki
6. Dark Grey
7. Grey
8. Black
9. Light Pink
10. Pink
11. Magenta
12. Purple
13. Yellow
14. Gold
15. Orange
16. Red
17. Lime
18. Palm
19. Green
20. Forest
21. Violet
22. Royal
23. Blue
24. Teal

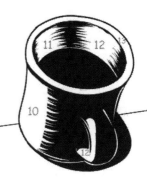

1. Dark Brown
2. Brown
3. Light Brown
4. Tan
5. Khaki
6. Dark Grey
7. Grey
8. Black
9. Light Pink
10. Pink
11. Magenta
12. Purple
13. Yellow
14. Gold
15. Orange
16. Red
17. Lime
18. Palm
19. Green
20. Forest
21. Violet
22. Royal
23. Blue
24. Teal

1. Dark Brown
2. Brown
3. Light Brown
4. Tan
5. Khaki
6. Dark Grey
7. Grey
8. Black
9. Light Pink
10. Pink
11. Magenta
12. Purple
13. Yellow
14. Gold
15. Orange
16. Red
17. Lime
18. Palm
19. Green
20. Forest
21. Violet
22. Royal
23. Blue
24. Teal

I regret NOTHING!

1. Dark Brown
2. Brown
3. Light Brown
4. Tan
5. Khaki
6. Dark Grey
7. Grey
8. Black
9. Light Pink
10. Pink
11. Magenta
12. Purple
13. Yellow
14. Gold
15. Orange
16. Red
17. Lime
18. Palm
19. Green
20. Forest
21. Violet
22. Royal
23. Blue
24. Teal

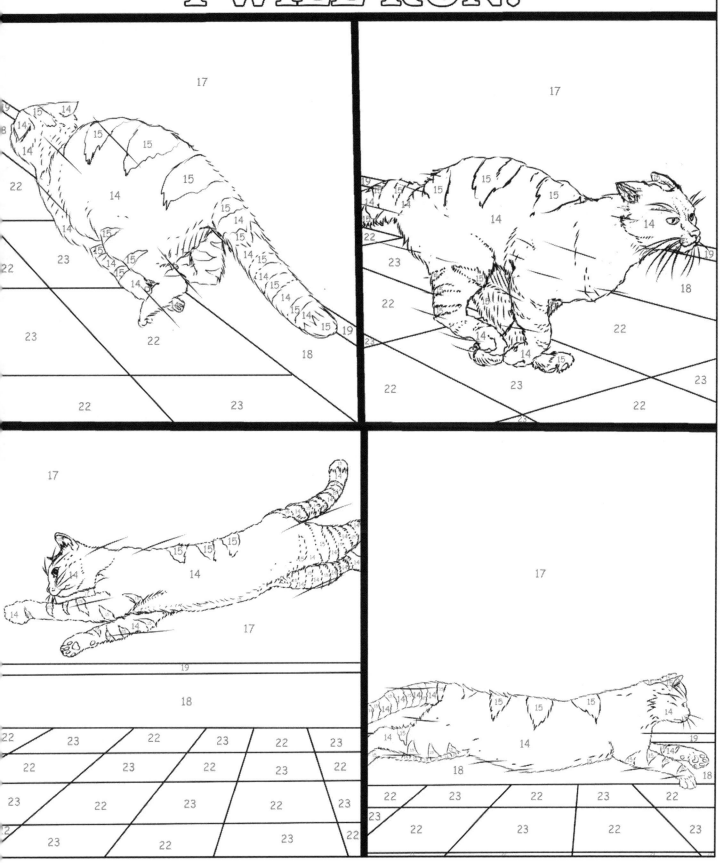

1. Dark Brown
2. Brown
3. Light Brown
4. Tan
5. Khaki
6. Dark Grey
7. Grey
8. Black
9. Light Pink
10. Pink
11. Magenta
12. Purple
13. Yellow
14. Gold
15. Orange
16. Red
17. Lime
18. Palm
19. Green
20. Forest
21. Violet
22. Royal
23. Blue
24. Teal

1. Dark Brown
2. Brown
3. Light Brown
4. Tan
5. Khaki
6. Dark Grey
7. Grey
8. Black
9. Light Pink
10. Pink
11. Magenta
12. Purple
13. Yellow
14. Gold
15. Orange
16. Red
17. Lime
18. Palm
19. Green
20. Forest
21. Violet
22. Royal
23. Blue
24. Teal

Happy Birthday, ass wipe.

1. Dark Brown
2. Brown
3. Light Brown
4. Tan
5. Khaki
6. Dark Grey
7. Grey
8. Black
9. Light Pink
10. Pink
11. Magenta
12. Purple
13. Yellow
14. Gold
15. Orange
16. Red
17. Lime
18. Palm
19. Green
20. Forest
21. Violet
22. Royal
23. Blue
24. Teal

1. Dark Brown
2. Brown
3. Light Brown
4. Tan
5. Khaki
6. Dark Grey
7. Grey
8. Black
9. Light Pink
10. Pink
11. Magenta
12. Purple
13. Yellow
14. Gold
15. Orange
16. Red
17. Lime
18. Palm
19. Green
20. Forest
21. Violet
22. Royal
23. Blue
24. Teal

1. Dark Brown
2. Brown
3. Light Brown
4. Tan
5. Khaki
6. Dark Grey
7. Grey
8. Black
9. Light Pink
10. Pink
11. Magenta
12. Purple
13. Yellow
14. Gold
15. Orange
16. Red
17. Lime
18. Palm
19. Green
20. Forest
21. Violet
22. Royal
23. Blue
24. Teal

1. Dark Brown
2. Brown
3. Light Brown
4. Tan
5. Khaki
6. Dark Grey
7. Grey
8. Black
9. Light Pink
10. Pink
11. Magenta
12. Purple
13. Yellow
14. Gold
15. Orange
16. Red
17. Lime
18. Palm
19. Green
20. Forest
21. Violet
22. Royal
23. Blue
24. Teal

I don't always tear up your toilet paper. But when I do I make sure it's your last roll.

1. Dark Brown
2. Brown
3. Light Brown
4. Tan
5. Khaki
6. Dark Grey
7. Grey
8. Black
9. Light Pink
10. Pink
11. Magenta
12. Purple
13. Yellow
14. Gold
15. Orange
16. Red
17. Lime
18. Palm
19. Green
20. Forest
21. Violet
22. Royal
23. Blue
24. Teal

1. Dark Brown
2. Brown
3. Light Brown
4. Tan
5. Khaki
6. Dark Grey
7. Grey
8. Black
9. Light Pink
10. Pink
11. Magenta
12. Purple
13. Yellow
14. Gold
15. Orange
16. Red
17. Lime
18. Palm
19. Green
20. Forest
21. Violet
22. Royal
23. Blue
24. Teal

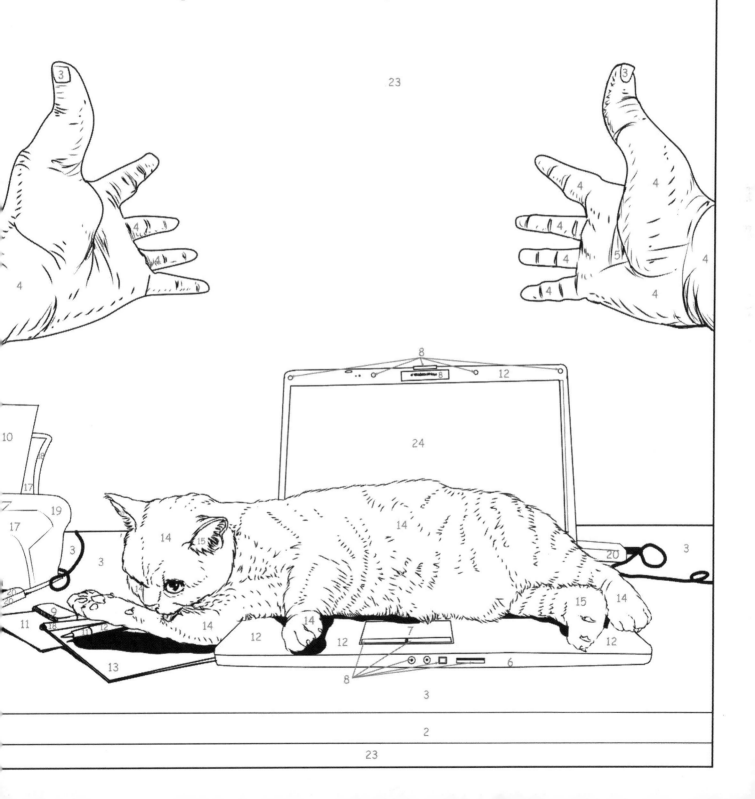

1. Dark Brown
2. Brown
3. Light Brown
4. Tan
5. Khaki
6. Dark Grey
7. Grey
8. Black
9. Light Pink
10. Pink
11. Magenta
12. Purple
13. Yellow
14. Gold
15. Orange
16. Red
17. Lime
18. Palm
19. Green
20. Forest
21. Violet
22. Royal
23. Blue
24. Teal

1. Dark Brown
2. Brown
3. Light Brown
4. Tan
5. Khaki
6. Dark Grey
7. Grey
8. Black
9. Light Pink
10. Pink
11. Magenta
12. Purple
13. Yellow
14. Gold
15. Orange
16. Red
17. Lime
18. Palm
19. Green
20. Forest
21. Violet
22. Royal
23. Blue
24. Teal

You may have a cat or plants. NOT BOTH.

1. Dark Brown
2. Brown
3. Light Brown
4. Tan
5. Khaki
6. Dark Grey
7. Grey
8. Black
9. Light Pink
10. Pink
11. Magenta
12. Purple
13. Yellow
14. Gold
15. Orange
16. Red
17. Lime
18. Palm
19. Green
20. Forest
21. Violet
22. Royal
23. Blue
24. Teal

Oh, you just washed these? Does it look like I give a shit?

1. Dark Brown
2. Brown
3. Light Brown
4. Tan
5. Khaki
6. Dark Grey
7. Grey
8. Black
9. Light Pink
10. Pink
11. Magenta
12. Purple
13. Yellow
14. Gold
15. Orange
16. Red
17. Lime
18. Palm
19. Green
20. Forest
21. Violet
22. Royal
23. Blue
24. Teal

1. Dark Brown
2. Brown
3. Light Brown
4. Tan
5. Khaki
6. Dark Grey
7. Grey
8. Black
9. Light Pink
10. Pink
11. Magenta
12. Purple
13. Yellow
14. Gold
15. Orange
16. Red
17. Lime
18. Palm
19. Green
20. Forest
21. Violet
22. Royal
23. Blue
24. Teal

Thank you for supporting
ZenMaster Coloring Books!

I aim to make sure my customers have the most enjoyable and relaxing coloring experience possible and I would love to hear your feedback!

Please leave a review on Amazon and follow me on facebook for updates and free coloring pages!

https://www.facebook.com/zenmastercoloringbooks/

check out more of my books at:

amazon.com/author/zenmastercoloringbooks

Free Bonus Page!
from:

UNICORNS
a day in the life
raunchy, sweary, and fabulous

https://amzn.com/1539983722

also available in
color by numbers version!

https://amzn.com/1979961891

Free Bonus Page!
from:

Happy Hour
Adult Coloring Book

https://amzn.com/1539662462

Also available in color by numbers!!
https://amzn.com/1976119944

BONUS PAGE! From "Zen Coloring Notebook"

Made in the USA
Columbia, SC
09 December 2018